for the young makers among us (and those who love them).—B.K.

This book owes a great debt of gratitude
to Helen Elletson of the William Morris Society,
who took the time to study our pages and help us avoid errors.
We are so grateful to Helen and indeed to the entire society,
which preserves the William Morris legacy.

for my Mother, a lover of beautiful things,
and my precious Jad, Mai, and Richard, who always support me
and have done so through every step of illustrating this book.
Thank you. x—M.S.

Text © 2022 Beth Kephart
Illustrations © 2022 Melodie Stacey

Book design by Melissa Nelson Greenberg

Published in 2022 by CAMERON + COMPANY, a division of ABRAMS.

Library of Congress Cataloging-in-Publication Data available.
ISBN: 978-1-951836-33-7

Printed in China

10 9 8 7 6 5 4 3 2 1
CAMERON KIDS is an imprint of CAMERON + COMPANY

CAMERON + COMPANY
Petaluma, California
www.cameronbooks.com

BEAUTIFUL USEFUL THINGS

What William Morris Made

Beth Kephart & Melodie Stacey

cameron kids

When William Morris was a boy,
his world was a beautiful thing.

In the cool curves of forest shadows
there were mysteries and insect wings,
slivered creeks and towers of trees,
and a boy winning gallant victories.

Nature was the best amazement—
flowers alive on twisted vines,
plums turning blue in the afternoon shade,

the sunflower and its fringe
attracting butterflies and bees.

Every one thing was part of another something—
the leaf, a part of the stem;
the bird, a part of the song;
the garden, a part of the house;
the house, a place for people to love and to live,
to meet and to think.

It takes a long time for a tree to become a tree,
for a vine to twine,
for a flower to bloom,
for a thread to become a tapestry.

The older William grew,
and the more he saw,
the more he wanted
to honor beauty
by making beautiful things.

By making beautiful *useful* things.

"Have nothing in your houses that you do
not know to be useful or believe to be beautiful,"
William said,
and so, with his friends, he began—

to sketch, to paint, to knot, to sew,
to carve, to fold, to hold,
to shape, to cut, to loom, to know
what the hands could do
when the eyes would see.

Meanwhile, inside factories all around Britain,
textiles and dishes, tables and chairs
were being mass-produced—
one thing looking just like the next thing,
ordinary and cheap.

The skies filled with smoke.
The rivers clogged with waste.
The forests thinned.

But in William's workshop,
each pattern, wallpaper, tapestry, and rug,
each stained-glass window
was conceived by the heart and made by hand.

Each thing took time
and love—
looked like time and love.

The older William grew,
the more he saw.
He traveled far,
visiting old cathedrals and countrysides,
farmers' hills,
riverbanks,
waterfalls.

Across Britain, across France,
to Iceland he went, where,
on the back of a pony,
he found a fjord,
a lava bed,
a garden of angelica.

From here and from there
he brought his discoveries home—
big books beneath his arms,
his own stories in his head.
One word leading to the next word,
to the next sentence,
just like a seed leads to a stalk
leads to a bloom.

William thought about how books, too,
might become beautiful useful things.
One book made at a time with care,
by hand.

There could be no beautiful books without paper,
so William procured the very best.

There could be no beautiful books without ink,
so William sought out the blackest of inks.

Then there were the letters—
his version of A,
his version of B,
his version of C,
each letter and mark telling a story.

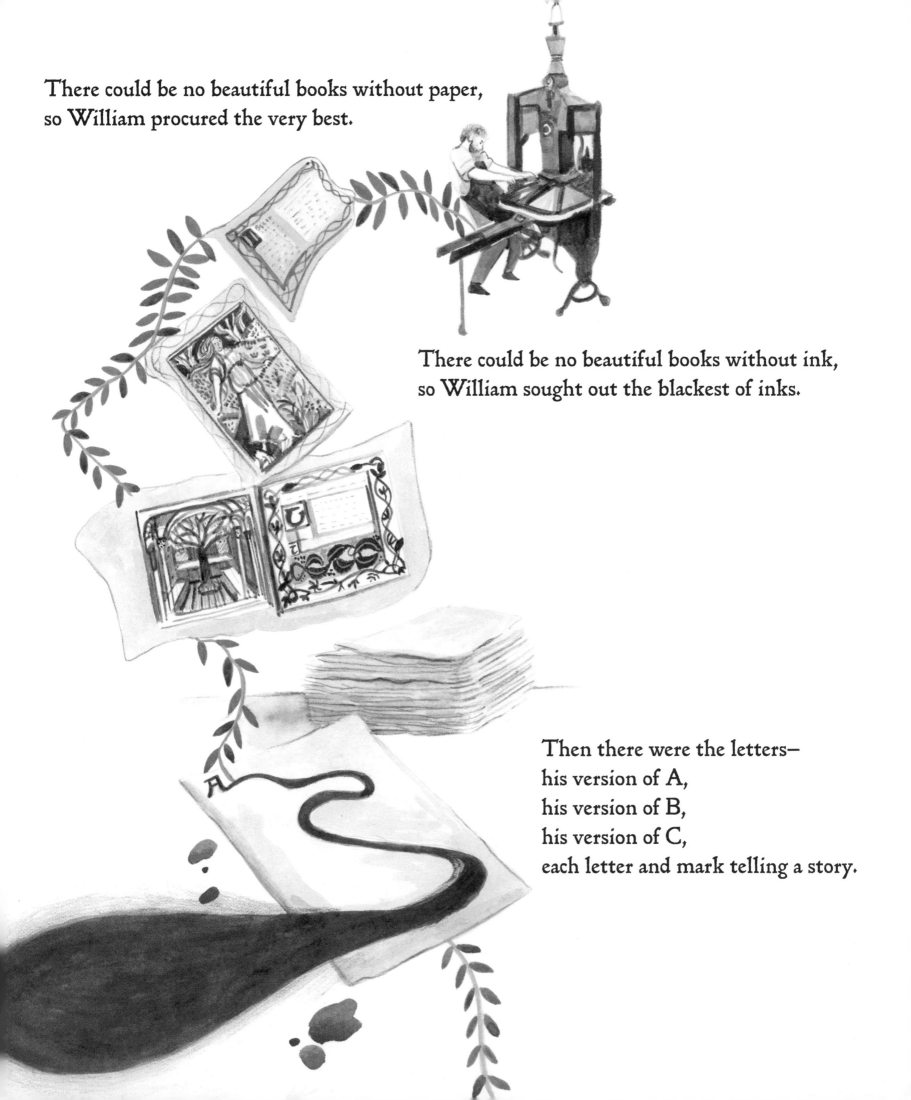

A B C D

E F G H

I J K L'

M N O P

There could be no beautiful books without
some really beautiful thinking
about how much space each letter needed
and how much room each sentence wanted.
A beautiful book would have to be
engaging but also easy to read,
page by page.

Pause . . .

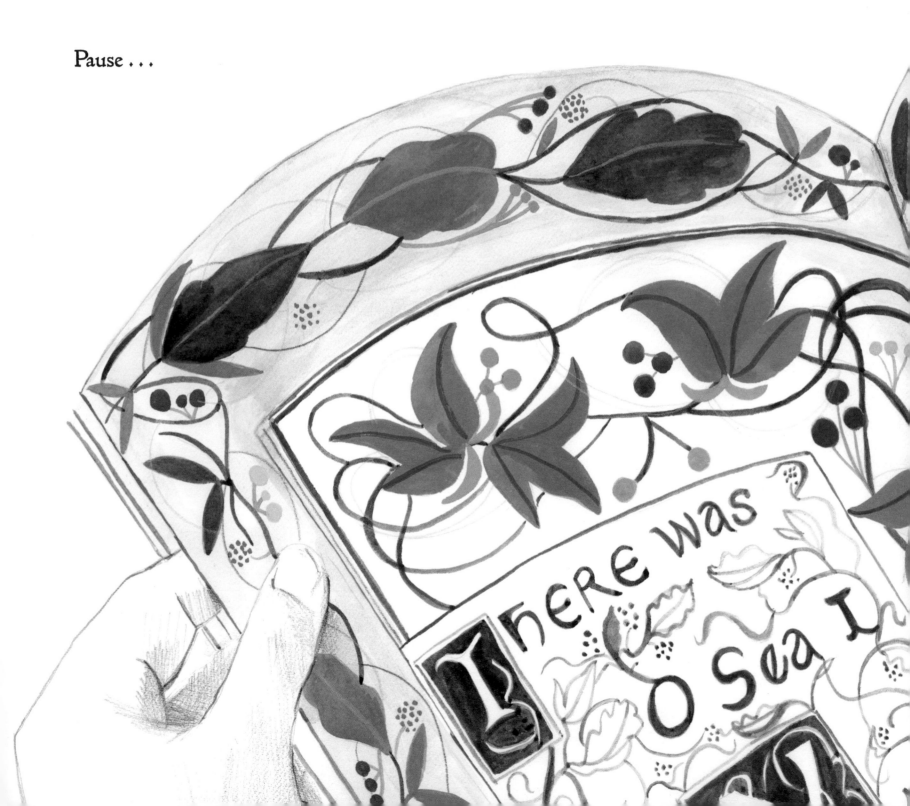

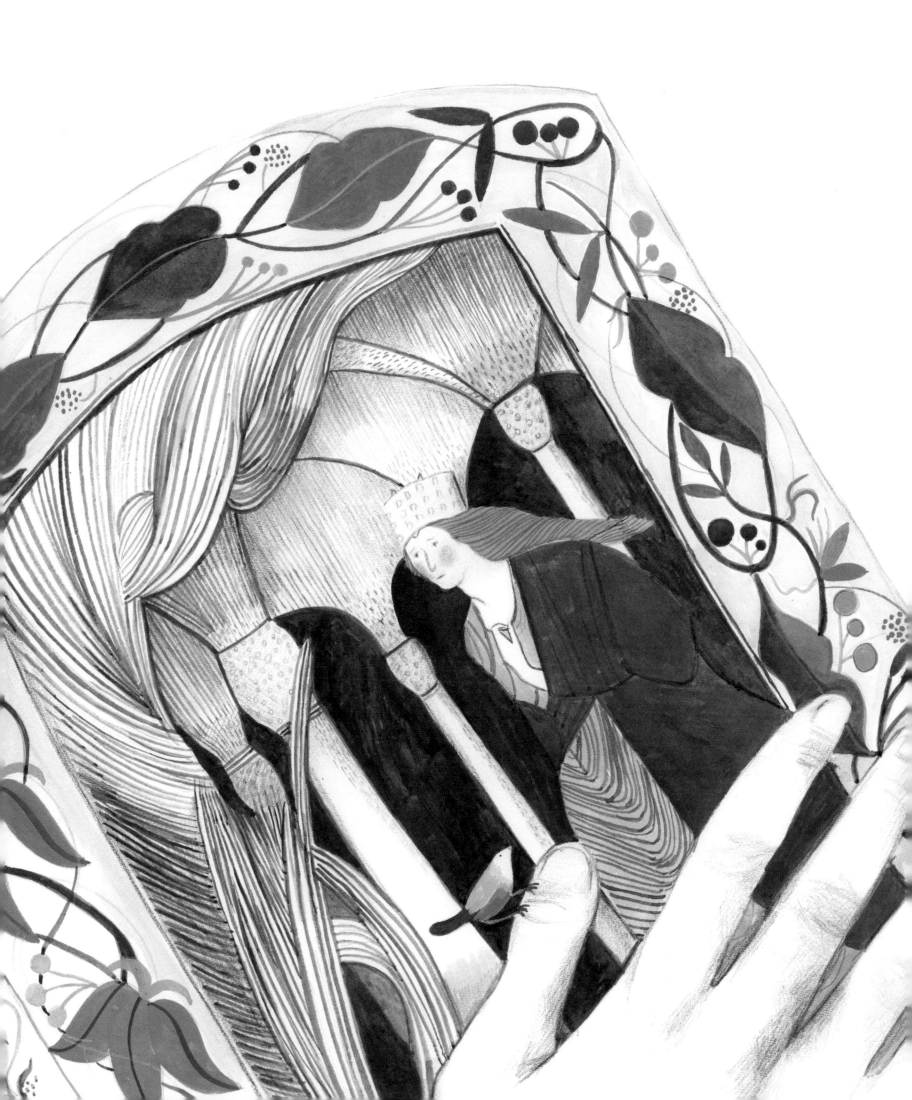

Picture.
Story.

William kept on making
beautiful useful things,
right until the end—
this writer, scholar, artist,
activist, bookman
who understood how beauty begins—
vine to twine,
stalk to bloom,
thread to tapestry,
letter to word to page—

each story circling back
to where it once began.

Strawberry Thief printed cotton, 1883

by William Morris

© The William Morris Society

AUTHOR'S NOTE

Born to a prosperous English family, William Morris (1834–1896) became a poet, a painter, a historic preservationist, an activist, an environmentalist, and a cocreator and purveyor of stained-glass windows, wallpaper, furniture, fabrics, carpets, and many other things. He taught himself the crafts of the Middle Ages and brought them to his Victorian age, collaborating with men and women alike to fill homes and churches with genuinely beautiful creations, and to help lay the foundation for the Arts and Crafts Movement. His wife, Jane, was both an artist's model and a master embroiderer. His two daughters, Jenny and May, learned to embroider professionally as young girls; Jenny would eventually be diagnosed with acute epilepsy while May would go onto become a multitalented artist who carried parts of her father's legacy forward. Toward the end of his life, Morris turned to designing and making books for his Kelmscott Press—creating new fonts inspired by old-style type, demanding the blackest ink, and layering art into the pages.

If Morris did, as it was said, the work of more than ten men, he was perhaps most famous for urging others to see art and those things produced by hand as central to our lives, our joy, our communities. He despaired over a society divided into those who work in the factories and those who buy what the factories produce. He insisted that when we surround ourselves with things that matter—things produced with care—we live more complete lives and take better care of our world.

When I was working on this book, I liked to imagine Morris nearby—his fingertips stained with ink, his shirt smelling of dye, his beard unruly. I imagined him asking us to stop, to think, to look, to wonder about what we might do to create a more meaningful existence. Watch the flower grow, he might say. Watch the vine sneak up and over the wall, and twist, and drip, and curl. Watch the strawberry bloom. Watch the bird build the nest among the blooms. And then draw. And then write. And then make your own beautiful, useful thing.

ILLUSTRATOR'S NOTE

I have long admired William Morris, not only as a designer and maker, but as a person. I've admired his artistic vision, his love of beauty in all things, but also his philanthropy and his fight for better working conditions and pay for his employees. That his mark on design still resonates today is a testament to him and those he worked alongside, including his beloved daughter and accomplished embroiderer May Morris. In illustrating this book I was inspired both by his designs and the way they seem to recall patterns in nature from my childhood in the East Anglian countryside surrounded by woods and a wealth of wildflowers, but also his love of collaboration and the importance of family and friendship. It was an honor to document a small part of what he achieved.

Sources:

American Bookbinders Museum, www.bookbindersmuseum.org

The Cleveland Museum of Art, www.clevelandart.org

Byatt, A. S. *Peacock & Vine: On William Morris and Mariano Fortuny.* New York: Knopf, 2016.

MacCarthy, Fiona. *William Morris: A Life for Our Time.* New York: Faber and Faber Ltd., 2010.

Morris, William. *The Ideal Book.* University of Tampa Press, 2007.

Morris, William. *William Morris: Full-Color Patterns & Design.* Dover Publications, 1988.

Morris, William. *William Morris by Himself: Designs and Writings.* Edited by Gillian Naylor. Barnes & Noble, 2004.

The University of Maryland Libraries, www.lib.umd.edu